The *Titanic* Sets Sail

On April 10, 1912 excitement was in the air. Passengers were preparing to sail from Southampton, England, on the biggest ship in the world—the RMS *Titanic*. It weighed 52,310 tons, had nine decks, and was bigger than a fifteen-story building!

Some people called the *Titanic* a floating palace. It had a carved wood-and-iron staircase with a glass dome at the top. There was even a swimming pool for first-class passengers. Of course, not everyone traveled first class. There were only 325 people who did. Some were so wealthy, they even brought their servants along.

Second class was nice, too. The rooms had beds, sofas, **wardrobes**, dressing tables, and a **washbasin**. Over 280 people traveled second class.

Recreation of the Titanic's Grand Staircase

Passengers boarding the Titanic.

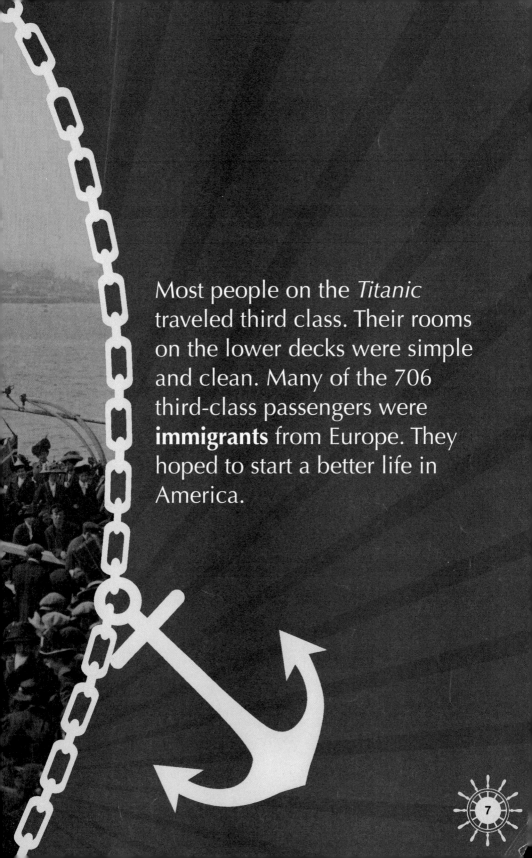

Most people on the *Titanic* traveled third class. Their rooms on the lower decks were simple and clean. Many of the 706 third-class passengers were **immigrants** from Europe. They hoped to start a better life in America.

The giant ship would cross the Atlantic and arrive in New York City in only four days. The Atlantic could be rough at times but no one worried. After all, the *Titanic* was unsinkable. Captain Edward John Smith said it was.

J. Bruce Ismay

So did the director of the White Star Line, the company that built the ship, J. Bruce Ismay, and the ship's designer, Thomas Andrews. In fact, they were all thrilled to be on board for its first voyage.

For the first few days, the *Titanic* sped smoothly ahead. People enjoyed the food, strolls on deck, and the cool but sunny weather.

But a little after 11:30 P.M. on April 14, everything changed. There was a jolt and a scraping sound. Then the engines stopped.

At first only a few people noticed what had happened. Many passengers were already in bed. Then suddenly, like wildfire, the word spread. The *Titanic* had hit an **iceberg**!

The compartments that were supposed to hold back water failed. And worst of all, there weren't enough lifeboats for everyone aboard. The law of the sea in those days didn't require any more than 16 lifeboats. That was only enough for a little over half of the passengers.

Painting of the Titanic's crash.

Evacuation scene from a movie about the Titanic.

Captain Smith ordered everyone to put on life jackets. He commanded the 16 lifeboats and four **collapsible boats** be lowered. Women and children were helped into the boats first.

People scrambled into the boats. But it was soon clear that there was only room for some of them.

The men in the **wireless room** tapped out the **distress signal** and the words: *We are sinking fast. Passengers being put into boats.*

They asked for help from any ship in the area but the closest ship to reply, the *Carpathia*, was three hours away. It would never arrive in time. The *Titanic* was already leaning into the sea.

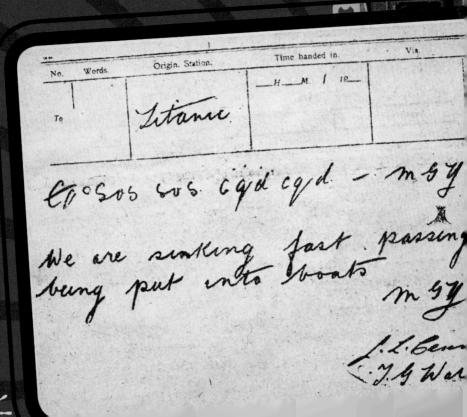

The Titanic's wireless room.

Painting of the Titanic *sinking.*

At 2:30 A.M., the great ship split in two. For twenty minutes the survivors in the lifeboats heard the cries of those who had fallen into the sea. Then there was a horrible silence.

At about 4:10 A.M., the *Carpathia* reached the first lifeboat. They helped the survivors aboard.

Survivors aboard the Carpathia.

The crew of the *Carpathia* offered people blankets, hot drinks, and comforting words. But it was hard to be comforted. It had been a terrible night. Over 1,500 women, children, and men had perished.

The *Carpathia* took several days through rough seas to reach New York. News of the disaster had already spread around

When the *Carpathia* arrived on April 18, friends and family waited at the dock. There were happy reunions and terrible sadness as people discovered who had survived the disaster and who had not.

The Titanic *makes headlines all over the world.*

Dr. Robert Ballard

Finding the *Titanic*

Over the years, many people have been fascinated by the story of the *Titanic*. An ocean explorer named Dr. Robert Ballard was one of them. "My lifelong dream," he said, "was to find this great ship." In 1985 Ballard and his crew sailed to a spot near where the *Titanic* sank. They used the *Argo*, a new underwater craft, to hunt for it.

On September 1, something amazing popped up on their video screen—pieces from the engine of the *Titanic*! Seventy-three years after the *Titanic* sank, Ballard and his crew found its remains. They also found beds, suitcase, dishes, and even shoes lying on the bottom of the sea.

The Argo

Bow of the shipwrecked Titanic

Robot combing through Titanic wreckage.

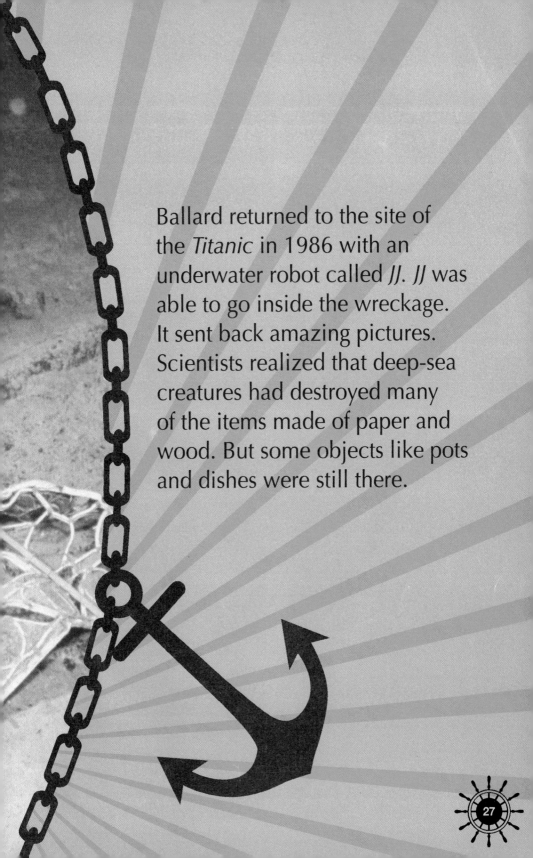

Ballard returned to the site of the *Titanic* in 1986 with an underwater robot called *JJ*. *JJ* was able to go inside the wreckage. It sent back amazing pictures. Scientists realized that deep-sea creatures had destroyed many of the items made of paper and wood. But some objects like pots and dishes were still there.

Ballard wanted to leave everything at the bottom of the sea as a memorial to those who lost their lives on the *Titanic*. Some people disagreed with him and brought up objects from the wreckage. Many others agree with Ballard and hope nothing else will be touched.

Coffee cup and plate recovered from the Titanic *shipwreck*

Millvina Dean

The Last Survivor

The last survivor of the *Titanic*, Millvina Dean, died in 2009. She had only been two months old when she sailed on the *Titanic* in third class with her family. Her father heard the ship scrape the iceberg. He hurried his family into one of the first lifeboats to leave the sinking ship. Millvina, her mother, and brother survived, but her father died in the disaster.

Telling the Story

Why are we still interested in the story c
ship that sank so long ago? What is it ab
the *Titanic* and its fate that has held the
attention for so long? Why have people
to movies about the *Titanic*, read books
the *Titanic*, and want to know more abo
what happened to the people aboard?

LEONARDO DiCAPRIO   KATE WINSLET

NOTHING ON EARTH
COULD COME BETWEEN THEM.

TITANIC

FROM THE DIRECTOR OF 'ALIENS', 'T2' AND 'TRUE LIES'

Perhaps it's because everyone thought the ship was unsinkable. Perhaps it's because it's a true story about how everything changed for over 2,000 people in only two hours. Or maybe it's because if you sailed on the *Titanic*, whether you were rich or poor, your life would never be the same after April 15th.

Glossary

Iceberg—A large floating chunk of ice that breaks off from a glacier

Collapsible boat—A boat with collapsible sides that can be stored easily on a ship

Distress signal—A message sent when there is trouble and help is needed

Immigrant—A person who moves permanently to a new country

Wardrobe—A closet where clothes are kept

Washbasin—A large bowl, or basin, to wash your hands and face

Wireless room—A room used to send messages using radio signals

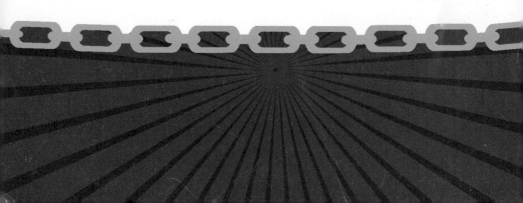